T0154873

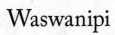

Waswanipi

JEAN-YVES SOUCY

Waswanipi

With an afterword by Romeo Saganash

translated from the French
by Peter McCambridge

Baraka
Books
Montréal

© Éditions du Boréal, Montréal, Québec, Canada 2020
Original title: *Waswanipi*

© Translation – Peter McCambridge

ISBN 978-1-77186-253-0 pbk; 978-1-77186-254-7 epub; 978-1-77186-255-4 pdf

Cover photo by Béatrice Tremblay
Cover by Maison 1608
Book design by Folio infographie
Proofreading by Barbara Rudnicka, Robin Philpot, Rachel Hewitt, Anne Lagacé Dowson
Glossary and verification of Cree vocabulary by Kevin Brousseau

Legal Deposit, 3rd quarter 2021
Bibliothèque et Archives nationales du Québec
Library and Archives Canada

Published by Baraka Books of Montreal

Printed and bound in Quebec
Trade Distribution & Returns
Canada – UTP Distribution: UTPdistribution.com
United States – Independent Publishers Group: IPGbook.com

We acknowledge the support from the Société de développement des entreprises culturelles (SODEC) and the Government of Quebec tax credit for book publishing administered by SODEC.

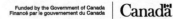

Jean-Yves Soucy began writing *Waswanipi* in September 2015. Only his passing in October 2017 prevented him from finishing it. The text was published at Carole Massé's suggestion.

Romeo Saganash, born in 1961 on the shores of a lake in his parents' tent near Waswanipi, is a former Deputy Grand Chief of the Grand Council of the Cree. He was MP for Abitibi-Baie James-Nunavik-Eeyou from 2011-2019.

Peter McCambridge is a Quebec City translator. His translation of Eric Dupont's *Songs for the Cold of Heart* was shortlisted for both the 2018 Giller Prize and the 2018 Governor General's Award for Translation.

"When the White man comes in my country
he leaves a trail of blood behind him."

Dee Brown, *Bury My Heart at Wounded Knee*

Prologue

When I was six years old, I would scale the hills behind my home in Amqui to look down over the Matapédia Valley. The fields at my feet ran down to the river, while the fields on the other side climbed the wooded hillside. I would think that were I able to hurl myself forward and soar high like the swallows, I would glide over the rooftops of houses and barns, over the road and the river below.

I would see the world from another point of view. As the crow flies. The age-old dream of humankind, a dream that never left me and that became reality for the first time in my teens.

I

1963, Waswanipi. The floatplane, a Beaver, pulls away from the water's surface with surprising ease for such a clumsy, barely aerodynamic plane. It's not so much my first flight, age eighteen, that impresses me as the thought that I have at last become a kind of bird. High in the air I discover the boreal forest I've walked through so many times. And this thick taiga—so dense that branches touch and obstruct one's view, so difficult to cross with its peat bogs, its streams, its plains of muskeg,* its beaver dams that impose long detours—looks from the air like a park ready to welcome anyone out for a stroll. You would think it was a scale model with its miniature

---

* Please see the Notes and Glossary at page 107.

trees! A living, breathing topographic map in three dimensions.

My nose pressed against the window, impervious to the vibrations of the cabin and the engine's deafening rumble, I feel as though I've been swept away to a new world. When I sent off my application to the Department of Lands and Forests in Amos for a summer job as a fire warden, I thought I'd find myself in a fire tower. There's one every fifty miles, teetering on a hill by a lake overlooked by the house that's home to two students every July and August; they scramble to the top of the tower every morning and spend their days keeping watch over the forest, scanning the horizon for any suspect signs of smoke.

But instead the government official asked me, in English, if I spoke English.

"My vocabulary is good, and I know the grammar, but my pronunciation leaves a lot to be desired. And I read it well, too."

With that I produced a paperback from my bag: *Lesson in Love*, the American translation of Émile Zola's *Pot-Bouille*. This seemed to impress him. The only library in my small town is to be found in the cathedral basement, and the only bookstore belongs to the staunchly

Catholic Clerics of Saint Viator: Balzac, let alone Zola, is nowhere in sight, both being on the Index! I found the book by the father of naturalism wrapped in a tourniquet at the newspaper and magazine store; I paid thirty-five cents for it, and still have it to this day.

Imagine blowing my own horn like that! The upshot was that I wouldn't be heading to a fire tower with another student, but to an equipment depot for forest fires. My initial disappointment evaporated when I learned my post was close to a Cree village, that we had two Cree guides, and that the work would consist of canoe patrols as well as maintaining supplies. In other words, I'd hit the jackpot!

Waswanipi Lake appears at last, a sprawling brown stain amid the lacklustre green of a sea of black spruce, 39.4 kilometres long by 13.4 kilometres wide, and covering 184.79 square kilometres. It is shaped a little like a crescent, either end leaning west, its belly swollen in the opposite direction. At one end the river arrives from the east, immediately leaving again for the north; an archipelago between the points where it comes in and goes out.

At the treeless tip of one of the islands, a smattering of wooden buildings painted white with red roofs, and irregular lines of rectangular tents, also white. The Beaver continues its journey, since the department's buildings are two kilometres further ahead, on another island right in the middle of the Waswanipi River, as it flows toward Gull Lake.

Once the two barrels of gasoline, the jerrycans of kerosene, the naphtha for the lights, a car battery, and our bags and supplies have been unloaded, the floatplane flies off again, leaving me and my companion alone on the floating dock. I'd thought I'd be spending the summer with a guy my age, but I've been paired with a fifty-year-old who looks like a little old man to my adolescent eyes. (Ah, how cruel youth can be! One day you will find that you were young at fifty...)

I'd like to head straight to the village, but we need to set a few things up first.

"You'll be fed up with the Indians soon enough," grumbles André, who thinks that he's in charge, the privilege that comes with age. "I know them. They're all the same: they're lazy and they steal."

My God, that got us off to a good start! And here was I, delighted to be working with two Crees. There are the Algonquins who live at Pikogan, near Amos, but I never had the opportunity to spend time with them. Perhaps I hold a romantic view of our land's original inhabitants and I'll become disillusioned as my companion expects; we'll see.

We'll be staying in a white house, its windows and doors framed by the same forest green that covers the roof. We walk into a large room that serves as kitchen, dining room, and living room. At the back, to the right, there's a bedroom with a bunk bed, and at the front of the house, a cubbyhole: the "office" where an enormous radio takes pride of place in its wooden case, decked out with dials, knobs, and levers, the very latest model... in 1930! This monster will be used to report daily to the Rapide-des-Cèdres office, to sound the alarm in the event of a forest fire, and to order the food the plane will bring us every two weeks (when it's not running behind schedule).

One thing our boss in Rapide-des-Cèdres has told us to do ASAP, his voice revealing his emotion as he entrusted us with the task, is to fly the Quebec flag outside. This will assert the province's authority in a part of the country the federal government has always managed as its own. Then we are to plug in the battery and get the little gasoline-powered generator up and running to charge it. Our electricity is for the radio only: we'll be cooking with the wood stove, using the oil lamps and a Coleman lantern for light. No fridge, of course, or even an icebox, just a shelf covered with a mosquito screen to keep the flies and the rodents away from the food. Don't I look smart with my two steaks, my eggs by the dozen, my ham, and my smoked sausages! My more seasoned "boss" has brought salt pork and cans of food. We decide to share my perishables before they spoil, then we'll make do with salt pork and canned meat: Klik, Kam, Paris Pâté, corned beef. We boil some of the eggs and conserve them in vinegar, which I can't stand. We'll just have to make the best of things.

There's a full moon that night, and the dogs from the reserve howl as one: a sublime chorus that, it seems to me, is the music of the land itself.

"Damn dogs!" André curses by way of good night, before closing the mosquito screen around his bunk.

"This is going to be just great," I think to myself. Sleep doesn't come easily, not because of the wolf-like howling, but because of the excitement I'm feeling.

The first morning, as I'm rolling a cigarette on the steps outside, a canoe comes into sight. It's carrying two men: our guides! I meet them on the dock and hold out a hand.

"Jean-Yves Soucy," I say, before adding, in response to the perplexed look on their faces: "John."

The man who had been sitting by the motor shakes my hand.

"Johnny... William Saganash. Him, Tommy Gull. He don't speak English."

I think he looks a little like my grandfather on the Soucy side, who always claimed to have Malecite blood in him. As for Tommy, he reminds me of the smiling face of my uncle, Albert Tremblay. So much for being far removed from my roots! Tommy points an index finger at me and asks:

"*Ochimaow?*"*

---

* Cree, as with other indigenous languages, uses the syllabic writing system invented in 1840 by James Evans. Since there is no official form of Cree in Latin characters, I have

"Are you the person in charge?" William translates.

"No. The boss..."

I point to the outhouse by the storage building and mime someone squatted over with a strained look on their face. It's then that I realize a laughing fit has nothing to do with race.

"*Misiou*," Tommy exclaims.

"He makes shit."

I repeat the expression over and over to Tommy. Amused, he corrects my pronunciation. "To take a shit," the first thing I've learned to say in Cree. I write down the word in the little black notebook I keep in the pocket of my wool shirt. The first entry in my Cree glossary! I can feel a rapport building between us, and since our "boss" tends to follow the same morning routine, William will often ask "*Tanta ochimaow?*" ("Where's the person in charge?") to get me to use the expression Tommy taught me. Fifty years later I find the words scribbled in my notebook, the pages yellowed and creased.

---

transcribed the words in a way that best reproduces, as it sounded to my francophone ear, the Cree pronunciation. *Publisher's note: please see Notes and Glossary for more information about the Cree words at page 107.*

First we take the canoes and the outboard motors from the boathouse. "24-foot Chestnut semi-freighter; 16-foot canvas canoe; 25-horsepower Johnson motor; 5-horsepower Evinrude motor." I check off the equipment that my companions carry to the river. In the coming days I will have to carry out a full inventory of the equipment in the storage building: so many hoses, so many knapsack tanks, so many pumps, round shovels, picks, axes, this, and that. My first encounter with the profusion of paperwork that will have to be produced to keep the pen-pushers happy, including a journal in which to note all our daily comings and goings: from where to where, from this time to that, with the number of miles travelled to be filled in under columns labelled "On foot," "On horseback," "By car," "By motorboat," "Rowed." Pointless reports, naturally, that I will quickly learn to falsify, passing off as inspections our fishing expeditions, Sunday picnics, lifts from the south shore given to Cree families arriving by train, and trips to carry back boards recovered from old logging camps. As well as a journey to Desmaraisville, where a grocery store sells beer, since our biggest boat is also used to accommodate the village Crees.

"Tomorrow… check… pumps," our "boss" instructs us, letting our guides leave mid-afternoon.

It's early and I insist that we visit the village. My companion isn't very enthusiastic about the idea, but since I say I can manage the small canoe by myself—a declaration of autonomy that visibly displeases him—he reluctantly agrees to accompany me in the semi-freighter. I can't wrap my head around his lack of interest, his lack of basic curiosity. The outboard won't start, no matter how much the boss grunts as he struggles with the starter cord. Without saying a word Tommy fiddles around with the motor, which then starts first time. A tough one for the boss to swallow!

The village runs five hundred metres along the shore, from the Hudson's Bay Company trading post at the southernmost tip to the chapel and the dispensary to the north. Between the two, a slew of tents and little wooden cabins arranged in what seems to amount to joyful anarchy. I'll later learn that the tents are arranged according to a semblance of hierarchy, parental ties, and friendship between families. William and Tommy land on the beach, where other canoes have been hauled away from the water, but we tie the big Chestnut to the dock outside the trading post, our first destination.

The Red Ensign, the flag of the British Navy, flutters in the breeze. The man in charge of the post, Mr. Lloyd, is happy to see us and invites us to his room for tea. A newcomer down from the Far North, where he married an "Eskimo," as we called the Inuit back then, he speaks with a British accent. His wife, a little on the plump side and several months pregnant, is absolutely radiant and offers us cookies she's made, sitting down at the table and asking us what we're doing and where we're from. When she leaves, the manager tells us she's bored to tears in the south, especially since she won't leave the house in case she runs into one of the "Indians" she fears and looks down on. There's no way she'll be giving birth with one of the Cree midwives; she'll have to be flown to the hospital in Senneterre because the nurse who works for the Department of Indian Affairs is only in Waswanipi over the summer.

While André continues to practice his English with the Brit in the kitchen, I go back to the trading post. It reminds me of the general stores villages used to have, where you could find absolutely anything, from bear traps to rolls of cotton. I shake my head in disbelief when I realize the food costs four to five times more than in the "south." Seeing my surprise, the store clerk—a young Cree—comes over and asks me in English if I think the prices are high. I nod and suggest that no one can afford that.

"When you have no choice," he says, with more than a little resignation in his voice.

We hit it off. His name is Simon Ottereyes. He's about the same age as I am, and goes to a residential school in Sault Ste. Marie, Ontario. Naturally enough I think of the university college in Rouyn, where I'll be boarding from September. Out of the blue he asks if I'd like to go waterskiing with him on Sunday afternoon. He can use the Hudson's Bay speedboat, which with its steering wheel and upholstered seats we call a yacht, and has no one to go with him.

"Everybody here is scared of skiing on water..."

I take him up on the invitation, not knowing that we'll develop a friendship over the weeks to come. It's he who teaches me the meaning of the name *Waswanipi*: "lights on the water."* It turns out that the Crees would use birch-bark torches for light as they harpooned sturgeon at night.

When my "boss" comes back to join me, we continue visiting the village. There are no motor vehicles in Waswanipi: the locals have beaten a well-trodden path that cuts the village in two lengthwise, running from the trading post to the chapel and the Government of Canada buildings. Narrow tracks on either side weave their way between the tents and the odd cabin.

Two women, visibly delighted to have visitors, come out onto the steps of the infirmary as they see us approach. The taller of the two has square shoulders, a stern look about her, and an urchin haircut; her virile handshake and that look that she won't be kowtowing to anyone lead me to believe that she's in charge. And the other one? The other one! A vision to sweep one off one's feet, an angel come down

---

* See Notes and Glossary at page 107.

from heaven, an impression that won't waver over the next two months. And everything—the nurse's rugged features, the rustic nature of their dwelling, the unforgiving surroundings—everything brings out the sweetness, the harmonious appearance, of this blonde angel, with a smile and a voice to match. Jean Ibbotson, a name I'll never forget again, and I have no memory for names.

The women invite us inside, where Jean puts the kettle on. More tea! I'd rather have coffee, but I'd drink hemlock if this wondrous beauty handed it to me. In love? No, I don't know her well enough. But I'm already beginning to wonder how I'll ever survive if I'm forever deprived of the happiness that comes from gazing at her. And while the older woman tells us about her life on the reserve, about their work, hers as a nurse, the other's as a missionary, I glance over at Jean, wondering what excuses I might find to come see her as often as possible, without the motives behind my regular appearances becoming too obvious. Since they live at the far end of the village, we can't very well say we were just passing by.

The nurse—who's in her early forties, I'd say—turns out to be warm and very nice. But her words are tinged by disillusionment with her Cree hosts and the doubts she has about the usefulness of working with them. Perhaps I'm jumping to baseless conclusions, but I think I can detect a hint of, if not contempt, then at least condescension toward the Crees, a certain paternalism (maternalism in her case?). I'll later come to realize that the people of Waswanipi distrust her, that they remain on their guard around her. She represents, after all, the Ottawa government; she is a symbol of this supreme authority that largely decides their fate.

For the time being, though, fascinated by the graceful ways of the missionary as she serves us tea, by the harmony of her every movement, I'm perfectly happy to bask in this feminine glow. To such an extent that, a separatist though I may be, I take no offence at the British flag pinned on the wall beside a portrait of Queen Elizabeth. And Jean is taking an interest in me! Asking about my studies, my plans. Her face lights up when I tell her I want to be a writer. Knowledge and books are essential to life in her eyes, second only to prayer and the Good Book itself. In an effort to impress her, I talk about the books I've been reading in English: Walter Scott, Dickens, and Hemingway. The final name elicits the beginnings of a grimace that, being civilized, she suppresses almost immediately. She holds up a Bible, enough reading for a lifetime.

My colleague is wiggling impatiently on his chair like a worm, rarely getting involved in a conversation he has difficulty following. A little in spite of myself, I feel sorry for him, since I get the impression that his lack of English isolates him and makes him feel inferior. Just as I was beginning to take a dislike to him, putting myself in his place lets me understand his vulnerability, humanizes him. All my life, my tendency to empathize, as well as a sensitive side that allows me to see what others are feeling, will stop me from ever truly hating anyone. Even those who might deserve it. Instead, it will help me reach out to people.

Still trying to figure out a way that will enable me to see the women regularly, I ask if they like fish. Their answer in the affirmative will provide me with an excuse for at least two visits a week, providing the pike and walleye are willing to cooperate.

As we're leaving, Jean tells me they read and comment on the Good Book every night after supper.

"Join us as often as you wish, Jannive."

I'm walking on air! *She* has asked *me* to come back, has given me a reason to. Is she attracted to me? Or does she only intend to "save my soul"? It doesn't matter. I have already disowned the religion of my forefathers and I'm quite prepared to abort my growing agnosticism.

We take the path back to the trading post. To our right, the tents and cabins are scattered almost right down to the water. Footpaths zigzag between them, marking the territories of many a dog. Outside his wood and tarpaper home, I recognize William, surrounded by a horde of children. He gives us a wave and we wave back, but the "boss" is sullen and wants to head straight back.

"We need to radio in our report."

If only it was that easy! We won't be able to get the antique up and running, or at least we won't be able to pick up the slightest signal, with no way of knowing if anyone can hear us. The following morning we'll realize we didn't connect the radio to the antenna up on the roof. Supper and the rest of the evening go by almost in silence, André giving up no more than a few terse words every time I try to start a conversation. He's sulking, it appears, and this childish behaviour leaves me puzzled. Once we're in bed behind our mosquito nets, once we've snuffed out the oil lamp, he snaps:

"Were you all laughing at me this morning?"

This outburst—more an accusation than a question, it seems to me, and something that's clearly been on his mind for a while—leaves me stunned. To defuse the situation, I end up bursting out laughing.

"I was trying to say 'take a shit' in Cree, and my pronunciation made our guides laugh. Why would they be laughing at you? They don't know you. They'd never even met you."

I think I've reassured him, if his grunt is anything to go by. So that's why he didn't want to visit William! Is he paranoid? If he's going to be like that, the next two months are going to be a struggle. A voice rasps among the distant barking and the shrill, piercing music of the mosquitoes that fills the room:

"And the two women are Protestants, not people to be spending time with. English, to boot…"

Is he a mind reader? At that very moment, I'd been thinking about Jean.

"Did you see the older one? A tomboy. Lesbians, that's for sure. Don't go wasting your time on them."

If he thinks that's going to put me off... A distant relative, a cousin's wife's sister we call "Auntie," has become close to our family. She works in a presbytery and visits us on Sunday afternoons. She always brings little treats with her and, after a chat with my mother, she plays board games with me and my brother, and we are very fond of this middle-aged woman, or this ageless woman, rather, who seems rather serious but who can be funny when the mood takes her. She often jokes about "her priests," all set in their bachelor ways, she maintains. My father insinuates that she has "leanings," that she works in a presbytery because the men there wear cassocks and lace surplices.

2

Either to punish me or to drive home his authority, my companion decrees that I am to stay home during the day while he carries out the canoe inspections with our guides.

"They'll walk all over you. They need a real boss," he says by way of explanation. "I'll soon bring them into line."

He comes back exhausted at the end of the day, so tired that he doesn't have the energy to help unload the canoe or pull it up over the logs onto the launching ramp. He walks inside bent over, one hand on the small of his back. William winks at me as he watches him go. At supper, my colleague grouses:

"Damn country. Portages everywhere, and long 'uns at that. And the black flies…"

On nights like these he doesn't even think about going to the village with me, and when I tell him the following week that we should take turns staying home, just like our boss at Rapide-des-Cèdres told us to, he doesn't protest. I suspect William and Tommy of taking the hardest routes to bring him into line. Working so many summers for the Department of Lands and Forest must have taught them how to deal with all kinds of White men, from the least competent and likeable or those who were willing to learn to pretentious types who thought themselves better than everybody else.

On my first day out with William and Tommy, they suggest we head over to Gull Lake, which is just as vast as Waswanipi Lake and some fifteen miles away. When I ask with a twinkle in my eye if there will be any portage involved, William allows himself the trace of a smile.

"Not today, tomorrow maybe…"

Tomorrow it's my colleague who will be going out with them. So I was right about their little game! The Chestnut negotiates its way between the tree-covered islands that separate the river on its way out of the lake, moving on to the higher riverbanks that run along a single stretch of river, rocks peeking out of the water.

"Rapids ahead."

Tommy is at the motor, William at the bow, and I'm in the middle, teetering on a narrow wooden crossbar that joins the gunwales. The river speeds up as the banks approach. I see Tommy throw a pinch of tobacco into the water. I give him a quizzical look, and he says a few words that William translates, adding an explanation of his own: Tommy believes in the spirits that live inside animals, plants, and all things. I ask if he believes the same thing. He slowly shakes his head, eyebrows furrowed, doubt tugging at his mouth and the stub of a cigarette that dangles from it. Judging by his sparkling eyes, I suspect he's about to deliver one of the befuddling replies he sometimes resorts to when he doesn't want to come down on one side or the other. William is a very clever man, an expert when it comes to human nature and being a pragmatist. He would have made an excellent diplomat.

"Why not?" he says eventually. "It's like having a spare oar…"

I had pictured William at the bow, keeping watch over the rocks below, but he turns his back on our destination and lights a smoke, indifferent to the canoe's jolts in the early swirl. Perhaps it's intended to reassure me, to show that Tommy doesn't need anyone's help guiding us through the rapids as they begin to roar. I don't share his sense of calm and instead crane my neck, on the lookout for submerged rocks, until I remember that, perched there as I am, I'm obstructing the guide's view.

We don't have lifejackets, and Simon has already told me that no one in the village can swim apart from him. I can paddle around a bit, but I won't last five minutes in water as cold and tumultuous as this. *Alea jacta est*, as Caesar put it. I try to adopt William's detached attitude, stop staring at the rocks flashing past both sides of the canoe, and sit at the back, turning away from the rapids. I look over at Tommy with his imperturbable smile, as he uses the motor as a rudder. He leans his head to the port side, then to starboard to read the current, getting his bearings from landmarks, distinctively shaped rocks, bent tree trunks, and rock slides. Just like William did, I roll myself a cigarette and put on an air of calm that I don't really feel. I consider my little show to be a form of politeness, a sign of trust in my guides.

While the tips of the trees are ragged and buckled, the trees in the peat bogs reduced to bare trunks with no more than a tuft at the top, along the shoreline they stand straight, tall, and full. The river eventually spills into Gull Lake. No buildings in sight. It's enough to make one think it's the beginning of the world, back when man was nothing but an animal among animals, subject like them to the caprices of nature, not yet laying claim to be master of all before him, to own the land. And when I ask William who owns the lake and the surrounding forest, he furrows his thick brows above his wrinkled eyelids, and laughs:

"That's a White man's question! The land belongs to no one; we belong to it. We eat what it gives us, until the day it eats us."

He said it all perfectly calmly, as though he considered death to be part of life, part of a natural cycle. I nod my agreement and remain pensive, juggling the remarks I've just heard. Tommy studies the sky, the passing clouds, exchanges a few words with William, then opens it up; we speed across the lake until we reach the west shore a few miles away. William indicates our direction of travel.

"Olga Lake, then Matagami Lake."

We're at the same latitude as the mining town north of Amos where I once visited a cousin who was working there. In a clearing by the mouth of a large stream, we see the tent poles left behind by an old camp, a firepit surrounded by blackened stones, and a pile of logs chopped for the fire; fishing nets hang from the branches of a tall spruce; and, further on, there's a structure to dry the fish over. We haul the canoe up onto the shore, grab our fishing rods, and disappear into the forest down a narrow trail littered with fallen, worm-eaten tree trunks. The walk in the bush, like fishing, hunting, and the canoe trip, is performed in silence: we listen to the world around us, observe it, meditate on it. The time for conversation is during a break or over a bite to eat.

William points an index finger at the barely visible trail left by a hare through the moss, at moose droppings. Then Tommy shows me an animal in the bushy crown of a spruce tree and murmurs, "*Wapistan*." A marten I hadn't seen.

After a half-hour's walk through clouds of black flies, we reach our destination: a sequence of waterfalls peppered with ravines.

"*Massimakouish.* Trout," says William.

Beautiful, plump trout who bite in no time at all. My sense of wonder delights my companions, who have seen it all before. We fish for our lunch and catch enough to take care of supper for three households, too. I reel in four more for Jean and the nurse.

"*Nthkoyiniskwaw?*" Tommy asks with a laugh, pointing to the fish I'm setting aside.

"*Skwaw?*"

"The nurse," William explains. "*Kawichihat nthkoyiniskwaw*, her assistant. Gonna get married, Johnny?"

"No, she is already married… to God. I don't think He would appreciate it."

More and more often, my guides gently poke fun at me. William in particular has a deadpan sense of humour. Once my reply has been translated for Tommy, we have a good laugh and we move on.

Back at the canoe, around the fire where water for the tea is boiled in a little blackened pan, we roast the trout over alder branches. My companions are amused to see me with my thermos full of coffee. Having eaten our fill, we have a smoke, stretched out on the moss.

"Black flies don't bite you?" William asks in surprise.

"They don't bother me. Only moose flies."

I beam with satisfaction, as though personally responsible for an unexplained trait that has often earned me reproachful looks from friends who are being eaten alive despite slathering themselves with fly dope. The bugs circle around me but don't care for my flesh, and if by any chance a mosquito, black fly, or no-see-um should bite me, there's no inflammation or itching. A real blessing for a hunter and fisherman who spends time in parts of Quebec that are simply crawling with insects.

I use our break to ask William a little more about the spirits. Do they have names? Do they also live inside people? He consults Tommy, who replies at length with a rapid, monotonous delivery. There are *wapanisou* (spirit of the east), *shawanisou* (spirit of the south), *chiwatinmisou* (spirit of the north wind), and more. Each of us also has a spirit inside us: *mistapéou* (literally, "the great man"). I hesitate before asking William if he also believes in the great man; once again he answers the way a Jesuit might:

"*Mistapéou* or the soul… maybe the same thing?"

I get the impression the conversation is making him uncomfortable, and he goes straight into telling me how he used to lead the canoe brigades for the Hudson's Bay Company. In June up to fifteen or so canoes, each carrying two men, would leave Waswanipi laden down with furs purchased by the trading post since the previous fall. Their route first took them to Gull Lake, then on to Olga and Matagami Lakes. From there they would follow the Nottaway River down to James Bay, hugging the shoreline until they reached Fort Rupert* to the north. Close to three hundred miles in all. From Fort Rupert the pelts would be sent on to England by boat. And on the way back the canoes would carry goods to be traded the following winter. William would usually make two or three trips during the warm weather, before heading to his hunting ground with his family. But those days were gone. Heavy

---

* Founded by Zachariah Gillam and Médard Chouart Des Groseilliers in 1668. Today known as Waskaganish.

goods are now delivered to Waswanipi from Senneterre over the winter, while perishables arrive regularly by floatplane.

This first excursion is just like the two months to come: a carefree existence among a welcoming, steadfastly optimistic people who have a contagious thirst for life. I feel accepted in the village, where everyone knows me and says hello; even the countless dogs only sniff at my coattails, never more so than when I'm bringing fish to Jean and her companion. I thought I was coming to a new world, but now I gradually realize that it's a different civilization I'm being confronted with, as different from my own as Chinese civilization would be. It's different in how it conceives of the world, of time, and of the place given to humankind in the universe, by its definition of property, by the obligation to help each other. And by how its politics are organized. The band has a chief only at the behest of the federal government, so that it would have an individual it could speak to. Diom Blacksmith, who was elected band chief before the Second World War, doesn't even have the authority of a village mayor; as things stand, his work involves consulting others, finding a consensus or building a majority, and acting as community spokesperson in dealings with Ottawa. He's a well-respected man, and his opinion carries weight when it comes to running the village.

We work six days a week, taking Sundays off, when we let William have the Chestnut. After church he comes to visit us with the rest of his family. I've made a habit of having two dozen oranges delivered; I'm not crazy about them, but William's wife and the Saganash children can't get enough of the sugary, juicy fruit.* And I always have hard candies, too, which are just as popular. I have the most fun with the youngest child, a chubby, cheerful

---

* Publisher's note: Jane Saganash, William's daughter, remembers the oranges the author would bring and provided this account. *"It was a summer day. The door flap to the tent was pinned open and I could see inside. I vividly remember the bowl of oranges sitting on a table. The oranges looked so good! I had glimpsed the oranges from time to time from where I was outside. I kept begging my father to let me have one of those oranges! He finally gave in to my whining for some reason and said he would let his friend know that he took one of the oranges. To my surprise, when the man returned that day he started giving out the oranges to us children, but he was short one orange! Of course, my parents reminded me that I had already eaten my orange and I was not getting another one. I can still taste that orange when I reminisce!"*

little baby who's not yet two; he runs over whenever he sees me, stretching out his arms so I'll bounce him on my knee, and rummaging around in my shirt pocket where I've hidden something sweet for him. We'll all head out for a picnic from time to time, to a spot where we've found raspberries, blueberries, cloudberries, and more.

Even our "boss" is in a state of grace on Sundays. Overcoming his prejudice, André comes with us, revealing himself to be perfectly pleasant company, no doubt savouring the good-natured, family feel of our outings. I have to admit that the old grump is starting to show a softer side as the weeks go by, especially since an inflamed sciatic nerve has gotten the better of him. It happened one day when he was keeping watch back at camp. Our little house and its outbuildings occupy a large rectangle, where the grass, which had been short when we arrived, had grown into hay that now reached above knee height; André had decided to take a scythe to it. When we got back that afternoon only a tiny crescent had been cut, and the large scythe was leaning against the house. The poor guy had trapped a nerve or slipped a disc, clutching the small of his back as he walked and moaning at the slightest movement. There was no way he would be able to sit at the back of the canoe, allowing himself to be rocked by the waves, or hobbling down trails.

We all stayed back the following day. Tommy gave the scythe a try, but not with much success: even though he can carry more than one hundred pounds over long portages without so much as stopping to catch his breath, he was quickly exhausted. William fared no better. So now it's up to me, the rookie, to make a name for myself. Back when I spent my summers in Sainte-Irène, my uncle Albert had taught me how to handle a scythe, how to balance the crescent-shaped tool by relying on weight rather than muscle. A cursory examination of the blade reveals it to be dangerously dull. So I spit on the stone and begin sharpening the wire that will make the scythe razor sharp. A sway of the torso, a slight rotation of the pelvis, legs steady: the scythe flattens a strip of hay; a step to my right as the blade comes back, balance, and a new strip falls. My companions are watching me, impressed. In a short time, I've already cut more grass than the three of them put together, and I'm not tired yet. I stop all the same at the edge of the forest for a cigarette with them. I make sure to remain unruffled by their appreciative remarks, but inwardly I'm jubilant: at last here's something I'm the best at!

I've never been one to rejoice in other people's misfortunes, apart from this one time. André is out of commission for a month, staying back at camp to keep watch, aside from trips into the village and family outings on Sundays. I'd been baffled he'd brought only essentials with him—no books, magazines, crosswords, or packs of cards—so I'm pleasantly surprised to see him with his woodworking tools: knife, handsaw, plane, chisel, metal ruler, wood glue, sandpaper. He's gone to a lot of trouble to build a miniature house. Not the easy way, using plywood for the sides, but painstakingly making the beams and boards by hand, all to scale. It's impressive, and I don't think twice about telling him as much.

It's only taken an inflamed nerve to make him more accommodating, bordering on friendly. And when he complains there's no ice left to treat his aches and pains, I let our guides know. Tommy and William consult, and soon we're heading into the village, where they chat to several men.

It's settled: we're on our way to the ice-house, a sort of square, doorless log cabin, with neither windows nor roof. It was filled with water over the winter, forming a two-metre-high block of ice. Covered in a thick layer of insulating sawdust, the ice will last all summer; this is where they store the fish that are .picked up by floatplane twice weekly. Work being hard to find in these parts, the men in the village fish commercially with nets on the lake since sources of livelihood are in short supply over the summer months. We chop off a few pieces of ice from the block. Our guides' generosity moves our *ochimaow*, who immediately begins preparing compresses. The strong smell of fish fills our house.

"I hope… bears not run after me…" says André, delighted.

It's the first time he's cracked a joke in three weeks, and we jump at the chance to show him we appreciate his sense of humour.

"We could use you to bait a bear trap," William chips in.

Since he has to wait on the translation into Cree, Tommy laughs belatedly, which cracks us all up again.

3

On my almost daily visits to the dispensary, I call in with either William or Tommy.
My Cree vocabulary has grown over time,
and I can now swap if not ideas then at least
pleasantries with the Gulls. But hand gestures
remain part of any attempt at conversation.
Husband and wife live in a prospector tent
that's stretched across a wooden structure,
complete with floor and two-foot-high walls.
When fall comes, they take down the tent
and bring it to the winter camp, putting it up
again the following spring. Mrs. Gull sewed
the tent's immaculate canvas by hand.

When I stop by, she's often at the stove,
which is outside so as not to overheat their
home. Short and stout, she's wearing a flo-
ral dress, a black sweater, a multicoloured

headscarf, and moccasins embroidered with glass beads. Memory can be a strange thing: I can no longer recall if the couple didn't have children or if their children had left the nest, but I can exactly remember the taste of the stew the woman was cooking, the smell of smoke given off by the leather strips hanging from the back wall, and even the tone of her voice when she welcomed me.

"*Kwei*, Johnny."

And her tender smile, the warmth in her eyes. Which leads me to believe that she missed her children being around. There was a lot of affection between the three of us, an inexplicable feeling that managed without words. One day the lady hands me a piece of wrapping paper and a lead pencil, motioning for me to take off my shoe and draw around my foot.

"*Mouswiyanmichisin, mouswiyanmichisin*," she explains.

I rack my brains, and then it comes to me. Making a set of antlers by placing my hands on either side of my head, I ask:

"*Mous... Napamous?*"

Tommy nods, then points to the moccasin he's wearing:

"*Mischisin.*"

"*Mouswiyanmichisin,*" she repeats, her face lighting up.

Moose-hide moccasins! I'd been dreaming of owning a pair. And I'm elated we were able to talk and make ourselves understood. Largely thanks to Simon's lessons. I learn words and their meanings from my guides, but it's Simon who teaches me the basics of Cree grammar. To signify that something is small, for example, you just need to add the suffix *-oush*, *-sh*, or *-ish* to the noun. That's how I was able to "discover" for myself what to call the pups that belong to Tommy's dog. I took the noun *atim*, "dog," and added *-oush*:

"*Atimoush?*" I asked, pointing to a pup.

"*Inhin,*" he replied, visibly delighted by my progress.

Since he speaks very good English, Simon understands the importance of grammar and the rules that give a language its structure. Most Cree words, for example, are verbs, and they have no infinitive: they always agree with personal pronouns. "Man" is *nipiou*, which means "he's a man." There's no feminine or masculine gender—the third person is neuter—but the concept of female and male does exist and is indicated using a prefix: *napa-mous* is a male moose; *nousamous*, a female. No gender, but two categories: animate and inanimate. Pronunciation is key, especially for the length of vowels. In this way *nipi* can mean "water" or "leaf," depending on whether or not the final vowel is drawn out. The plural of inanimate nouns is formed by adding *-a* or *-wa* to the word, or by lengthening the final vowel: *sipi*, "a river"; *sipii*, "rivers."

All of which is to say that the language is a complex one to master; it's rich and supple, favourable to neologisms. It's a melodious language that the Eeyou (Eeyouch)* in the singular) speak quickly, with plenty of elisions that tend to disconcert novice speakers. And what's more, they speak in low voices, a habit that perhaps comes from sharing a tent with many others or from hunting whenever they walk through the forest. The nurse has explained to me that the Crees avoid people who speak loudly, who shout at the top of their voices.

Since I suspect Mrs. Gull won't take any money for the moccasins, I order four pounds

---

* As well as being the noun the Crees use to refer to themselves, the word also means "human being." (Please see Notes and Glossary on Page 107.)

of Salada tea, bricks of it wrapped in thick foil. And I don't give them to her in exchange for the moccasins, but instead as a gift a few days later.

"How do you perceive time?"

My English is built around everyday life, and the same goes for William. It takes a lot of twisting and turning and paraphrasing to make my question intelligible, and William has to deliver his reply in a similar roundabout fashion. Our exchanges are therefore often laborious and require no small amount of patience, a quality that thankfully isn't lacking in my conversation partners.

William shares my question with Tommy, who laughs and briefly replies.

"Tommy asks where you find all those questions."

I also laugh and strike my chest with my index finger, towards my heart, a reply that Tommy seems to appreciate. He addresses me directly, making rolling motions with his hands.

"It's like the water in a river that flows slowly then speeds up in a rapid."

So time flows, then, and I think to myself that our concepts of the passage of time aren't all that different. Tommy speaks again, and William translates as best he can.

"The calm river is summer; the rapids, winter. Time passes more quickly in winter; we can do less."

Through our laborious conversation, I come to realize that for Tommy—and no doubt for William, too—time isn't an objective, outside measurement, but rather a perception that comes from within, organic and measured by the number of actions that can be performed over the course of a certain interval, from noon to sunset, say. Time therefore contains fewer actions in winter, when the days are shorter, and so it passes more quickly. What's more, time is not linear, but circular, cyclical, and we live in the present moment: yesterday is no more, tomorrow has not yet come.

The nurse told me that the Crees don't open up to White people, will reply no more than succinctly to questions, and keep their innermost thoughts and reflections to themselves and to their own people. I realize I have a special bond with my guides, no doubt because they consider me respectful and eager to learn.

William's reluctance to speak of religion, of conceptions pertaining to traditions and the world around us, which I first took to be a sense of propriety, I now consider to reveal a form of agnosticism: he won't choose between Christian faith and pantheist beliefs, modernity and tradition, instead reserving his judgment without coming down on either side. Since reaching this conclusion, I no longer ask him what *he* thinks after he translates Tommy's words for me. I get the impression he appreciates that, since now he derives more pleasure from trying to explain the secrets of his *bosom*,* who, unlike William, has no problem opening up to me.

As for William himself, he never passes up an opportunity to teach me all he can about life in the forest. Whenever I ask why he and Tommy always see the animals before I do, he replies that it's because I'm looking for them.

"The only animals you can see are by the water, in an old burn, or in a muskeg. The others are invisible."

There's no point trying to see the animals in their entirety, he adds, because they

---

* From the English, *bosom friend*

hide behind trees and bushes, rocks, anything that obstructs our view. Instead, you have to observe the landscape, spot movements, changes: a dark splotch disappearing between two tree trunks, that could be a moose or a bear. He teaches me how to look and reveals his hunting secrets. When I tell him how I wounded a moose two years previously and followed it in vain for a whole afternoon, he sets me straight: it's because I set out after it. A wounded animal, if it isn't followed, will lie down to rest; if it's left alone for at least an hour, it will lose its strength and no longer be able to flee. He also tells me about animals' curiosity, which will win out over caution or fear as long as they don't pick up our scent. These lessons were subsequently very useful to me, when out hunting moose, deer, and caribou or simply birdwatching.

Toward the end of July we head out to the southwestern corner of Waswanipi Lake to inspect an old burn that had been hit by fire three years earlier. Not for safety reasons, but to check on the blueberry bushes that have taken over the land cleared by the fire. We make our way up a narrow river as it meanders lazily, lined by thickets of alder and willow, behind which stand trembling aspen. William occasionally points out where the beavers will venture out onto the shoreline. At a bend in the water a stack of trees, their foliage still green, bars the river. They've fallen from both banks. The work of beavers? On either side of the water, we have our answer: a winding corridor, thirty metres wide, has been plowed through the forest. As though a gigantic run-away bulldozer had knocked down every tree in its path.

"*Yotinipiyou*. Tornado."

A tornado in Abitibi! Tommy remembers such a thing happening when he was young. There's no way through the tangle of tree trunks. We moor the canoes; we'll have to walk the rest of the way. But first we'll have to satisfy our curiosity. The trees have fallen towards the middle of the corridor, as though sucked up, the forest intact on either side. The aspen have been uprooted; others have seen their trunks snapped in two. The wind must have been very strong and concentrated. And the destruction goes on for as far as the eye can see. A tornado! A couple of weeks after a total eclipse of the sun. The summer of 1963 is decidedly spoiling me.

Each carrying a pail and a backpack, we take a moose trail that runs along a row of bushes by the river. The soggy trail winds its way between the aspen, occasionally overcome by a black muddy humus that's been churned up by hoofs. Here and there a darker thicket of conifers. Since early morning, Tommy, who's walking ahead of us, the .22 resting in the crook of his elbow, has been quiet and on edge; it's not like him. Suddenly he stands stock-still. We do the same as he cocks his rifle, steps forward another two paces, takes aim, and fires. Clack! A rustling of feathers. A spruce or Canada grouse falls from the branch where it had thought it was safely out of harm's way.

I try to hide my discomfort: hunting at the height of summer! It's not sportsmanlike... But would it be any more sportsmanlike in October? The futility of my reaction hits me. Here it's not about sport, but about subsistence, sometimes even survival. The Crees have lived in this forest for thousands of years and, on lands as vast as these, nomadic hunters have not upset the natural balance. While Tommy goes to pick up the bird, I ask William what's up with our companion.

"He had dreams."

And he believes dreams to be messages from the spirits announcing the future.

Before Tommy hangs the grouse from his thick canvas backpack, we take turns feeling the weight of the bird in our hands, its red eyebrow comb identifying it as a male. The body is still warm, and I imagine the aroma of roasted meat as I breathe in its scent. I'm momentarily consumed by the image of a golden chicken thigh with French fries!

Five minutes further on, I stop the others, point to a tamarack branch, and whisper:

"*Wapistan.*"

The two men nod and look impressed, but I suspect they saw it before I did and wanted to see what I was made of. Tommy corrects me:

"*Outchek.*"

"*Pekan.*"

My first *pekan.** It's true: the animal is a little on the large side for a marten. It disappears behind the trunk, and we continue on our way.

---

* A fisher (*Pekania pennanti)*

Judging by the sun, it's taken us a good hour to reach the burn. For as far as the eye can see, lush green vegetation covers the undulating soil from which spring the emaciated skeletons of blackened tree trunks. Fallen branches and calcinated trees have been piled up nearby to make way for the pumps and firefighting equipment, and a profusion of raspberry bushes now grows there, laden down with ripe fruit, while the ground disappears beneath a blue-berry sea. Without a word, all at once we turn to our right, where we've sensed something move: two hundred metres away, a mother bear with her cubs. She raises her head in our dir-ection—the wind has carried our scent—then scampers off, followed by her two little black balls. It's not the first time we've encountered a bear, and it's always a thrilling sight. Bears are a force of nature, special beings with a powerful spirit inside; they must be treated with respect when killed, even more so when eaten. William no longer seems uncomfortable reporting what Tommy has just said.

It's decided that we'll come back on Sunday with our families.

"*Pasho otchimasquaw, Johnny*," William laughs.

Our explosion of laughter is liable to set off another tornado. William's just told me to bring my woman! He's referring to the "manager-lady," our boss who's currently out of commission back at the camp, where he cooks and looks after our home. The joke is good natured; André has been pleasant company since he's embraced his homebody lifestyle. The previous week he even took up baking and handed out still-warm bread to our guides. He's told me that he spends his winters as a cook at the camps, a position known as a *bouilleux*, or boiler, since all the meat is served boiled, whatever the cut.

When our laughter dies down, I tell William:

"I could bring Jean, the missionary, instead."

He makes a face and becomes serious again.

"Let's keep things between us... And remember, God will not be glad if you fool around with his wife."

They go for the blueberries, while I head for the raspberries. And the prickly stems. Naturally enough they finish before I do, and they help me fill my pail. We cover each container with a piece of cloth, attaching it to the metal rim. Then we have lunch. On the burned-through ground we light a small fire from dry, charred wood to warm the water. Making tea is a ritual, a moment to be shared, and since I realized that, I've stopped bringing my thermos of coffee. Fresh supplies arrived yesterday, and now I have sliced bread that's not speckled with green mould, I treat everyone to buttered bread with thick slices of Kam.

"I wonder what kind of animal it was."

"It's better not to know…"

Once he's emptied a first cup of black tea, Tommy says:

"The world is changing."

It's more of a sigh than a mumble.

"What does he mean by that?"

"I know what he means," says William, who relays my question to our companion all the same.

The reply is long, a monologue delivered with sadness in his voice.

"The government takes away our children every fall and brings them back the following summer. School… They no longer go with their parents to the winter hunting grounds. They've stopped learning how to hunt, trap, and prepare the pelts. They no longer know how to live in the forest. They no longer know our traditions."

I've never known him to speak for such a long time and, once William has finished translating, Tommy adds:

"Being without traditions is like descending a rapid in a canoe without a motor and without a paddle."

Another pause, which he uses to light a cigarette with the glowing tip of a firebrand.

"We show them the best side of the White world. The ones who go to school no longer want to live off hunting and trapping. They have no ties to the land of their ancestors. They go off to work at camps or mines, like the White men, only they're not White men. And no longer *Eeyouch*."

I nod my head sadly to show him I understand, and we stay silent for a long time, drawing out the break with more cigarettes. We all turn over the words in our mind; our happy-go-lucky mood has upped and left.

"Johnny, aren't you going to ask what I think of it?" says William, a little irony in his voice.

"Please, tell me."

"The world has already changed, and it's changing faster and faster."

It's William's turn to launch into a long monologue, but he seems less despairing than Tommy. There's no turning back, he says. It's too late. The Crees can no longer live as they did before: there are more of them now, and their habitat has been divided up by logging camps, mines, and towns for the workers to live in. All of which disturbs the animals, and the roads bring in White hunters. There's no longer enough space, no longer enough animals to live in the forest as before. And with the price of fur constantly falling, there's no longer any money in trapping. Things are getting worse: The White man's world is growing, impinging on the Indigenous people's world. Lastly, school is perhaps a necessary evil. They need to know the White world, acquire their knowledge to be able to stand up to them, know how to negotiate with them. Not try to become White themselves, but learn a new way to live as Crees."

I'm expressing what he said succinctly, summarizing it, but their account was long and arduous, the words we were looking for failing to come to both William and me, and I'm upset at the language barrier that no doubt deprives me of much of my guides' thoughts, of their richness. And as William tells Tommy what he's just told me, I feel quite moved: these innermost thoughts, coming as they do on the back of more than a month of seeing each other on a daily basis, show the faith the two men have in me. As though they don't consider me altogether a White man.

Tommy doesn't seem entirely reassured by his friend's arguments, and I feel as though I can chip in with my two cents. I point out that for thousands of years the world has always been changing, even if that change came more slowly, and that their ancestors always managed to adapt, to alter their techniques, to modify their approaches, to develop new traditions. We mustn't lose hope.

When William is done translating me, Tommy gives me a friendly smile. Without adding a word or consulting each other, we put out the fire, gather up our belongings, and return to the canoe. Only once we are back in the canoe do we say another thing. William says we'll bring a chainsaw to clear the logjam; Tommy, that he'll bring his .303 rifle for the bears.

In the bay the river flows into, a black duck bobs around with her young: six ducklings who have already lost their down. William cuts the motor and as the canoe continues to drift, Tommy shoots the duck and two of the ducklings. He hands the .22 to William, who shoots two more. It's my turn. I slip a Long Rifle cartridge into the one-shot gun. Missed! I reload. Missed again! Fortunately, the two survivors want to stick with their family and don't stray from the bodies that are floating peacefully on the water. The rolling of the waves complicates the shot. Happily, the third shot is on target. Tommy motions for me to take aim when the waves tilt us in towards the birds, to roll back with the canoe while maintaining my position, and to shoot when the next movement brings the sight in front of the target. Click! First go, this time. Tommy picks up the game and begins handing it out: the spruce grouse, duck, and two ducklings for William; two ducklings each for me and him. The ducklings are about the size of a woodcock, their breasts already muscular from beating their wings as they run across the water's surface.

"In stew," William advises.

André will in fact cook the birds in a pot of pork and beans, simmering them all day, filling the kitchen with a delicious aroma but transforming it into such a steam room that we'll end up eating our meal outside on the dock.

To once again rid myself of my guilt I tell myself that the ducks, like the spruce grouse earlier, would no doubt have been killed by hunters from the south, not out of necessity, but just for "sport," while at least now they'll be filling hungry stomachs…

The following week, men from Waswanipi kill a moose, a two-year-old male. By the lake, between the beached canoes and the first tents, the animal is gutted surprisingly quickly, and while two women scratch at the underside of the pelt now spread out on the ground, the hunters carve up the carcass in the midst of a cloud of buzzing flies. Almost everyone who lives in the village, including us, forms a circle of delighted but serious faces. Even the little ones sitting in the front row seem contemplative, quieter still than during the Sunday service. It feels like taking part in a sacrificial ceremony that has a touch of magic about it: nature is offering up a feast to its children, assuring they survive for one more day.

In Matapédia from a young age I would look on as the pig was slaughtered in November, first stirring the pail of blood, then holding the pan that gathered the red flood streaming out of the wound. Once the precious liquid had been brought to the kitchen where the women would prepare the blood sausage, the animal was emptied of its organs, then the carcass was attached to a ladder that served as a stretcher and plunged into an enormous cast-iron pot (the same one used to make soap), where boiling water would wash the skin and make the bristles easier to shave.

"Every part of a pig is good," Uncle Albert would grin as he cut off chunks of lard from the barrel of brine.

The same words every year, as though to justify the killing. And it's true that nothing was lost: not the tripe, not the trotters, not the head. Everybody involved would list their favourite parts; my father's were the rouelle and the snout. Despite the pig's hideous squeals as it met its end—squeals that could be heard from the neighbouring farms—it was a joyous occasion as we looked ahead to a fine meal and got ready to indulge.

And once I turned ten it was I who gutted and prepared the partridges, hares, and groundhogs my father would kill; given my interest in biology, I'd dissect any dead animal I could lay my hands on. Which means that when I was sixteen, I was tasked with gutting the moose we had killed. We tend to imagine the entrails making a terrible stink, but unless you pierce the stomach or intestines, the carcass gives off a warm perfume of life: nothing is cleaner, nothing more sterile, than a body's insides.

The two hunters cut up the animal and proceeded to hand out the meat, following an order I couldn't figure out, an order that included us, the two White men from the next island over. André and I got a fine cut, a good five or six pounds of still-warm, dark red meat. Normally the meat would be left to "ripen" and age for two or three weeks, which proves impossible in warm weather with no methods of conservation.

That same evening we carve up our share into nice, thick slices that we barely roast in the pan. With no accompaniment, we devour the lot, leaving nothing for the next day; we'd missed fresh meat so much.

"I've never eaten anything so good," André sighs.

Sitting outside on the stoop, bellies full, we watch in silence as evening falls. We've even forgotten about our daily report. We'll say we had trouble with the battery.

4

There's to be a wedding in the village. The bride, having just spent two years in the United States with an American couple who are friends of her family, flies in with them on a floatplane. The day before the ceremony André and I head out early in the semi-freighter with our two guides and go to Desmaraisville, along the gravel road that runs between Senneterre and Chibougamau, some seven kilometres east of Waswanipi Lake. There's a grocery store that sells alcohol there, and we're off in search of plenty of beer for the wedding. The arrangements have been made by the bride's family, but White men have to pick it up since the Indigenous people aren't allowed to purchase alcohol and it's a criminal offence to sell it to them.

What if we're surprised and stopped by the police? Too bad! Besides, a spell behind bars will give me something to write about as a novelist. I say "novelist" rather than "budding novelist" because I wrote a novel two years previously, a book that spent four months idling in the offices of Les Éditions du Jour. The manuscript was returned to me with a letter from Jacques Hébert, explaining that the delay was because the reading committee couldn't make up its mind whether or not it should be published. Finally, he, the publisher, had decided to turn it down, and he outlined the reasons why on the three handwritten pages that followed. It was an early work, not quite there yet, and I would later regret having published it, he maintained. He encouraged me to keep on writing, saying that I had real talent. The letter often brought solace to me over the years to come, particularly when I was twenty-one and was again turned down by Alain Stanké, at Les Éditions de l'Homme, I believe.

No police officers in sight, the operation is concluded swiftly, and we don't hang around (you never know). André and I buy a case of beer each; we're not allowed to drink on the job and haven't touched a drop since we got here. The canoe is piled high, but you'd never know from the way it moves; which is just as well since the meandering river, full of shallows, requires some negotiating.

The trip has upset me. I've come to realize that the Crees, like the other First Peoples, are second-class citizens. Not even that: they're wards of the state that governs their lives, confines them to reserves, forbids them alcohol, takes their children away to residential schools and, in a word, infantilizes them. Simon has told me that the "Indians" didn't get the right to vote until 1960. Before that, in order to vote, they had to give up their Indian status, leave their reserve, assimilate. I wonder how many, in Waswanipi or elsewhere in the forest, voted in the previous year's elections. No one came to set up a polling station here, that's for sure! Besides, why would the Crees have come out to vote? They have their own political setup, their chiefs, and the issues at stake in federal elections are so far removed from their everyday concerns.

I recall the words Tommy and William spoke to me back at the burn, and they play on my mind. I don't know if it comes from having caught a glimpse of "civilization" (although if you ask me, Desmarais*ville* still has a ways to go before it can be considered a *ville*, or town), but I can almost physically feel how the world of the White man—my world—has us surrounded and is relentlessly moving in on us; how the still-wild world is shrinking. It's an oppressive, stifling feeling. William seems to think it's unavoidable, and he's most likely right. Just as Tommy is right to be sad at the traditions being lost.

I can see it in Simon: he's torn between traditional society and the White world he's spent time in since he was six years old. He's good at explaining the Cree language and societal norms to me, people's mentalities, but whenever I ask him about certain traditions my guides mention to me, like sweat lodges and shaking tents, Simon reduces them to bygone superstitions, old beliefs in spirits, legends invented around the fire. He also calls other traditions into question, such as the one that ensures the woman he will marry has been chosen long ago by his parents.* Simon

---

* He was a skirt-chaser, and I'd been surprised he hadn't paid more attention to one very pretty girl in particular. "She is my future wife. No hurry. I will spend my life with her," he'd replied.

is caught between two civilizations, straddling two chairs, and he's not the only member of his generation in this position. I wonder if they're the ones who will begin the rapid change that one day members of the First Nations will be subjected to.

The wedding is a happy affair, followed by a reception that André and I are invited to. There's plenty of alcohol to wash down the meal, which has the village in even higher spirits. When evening comes the old school holds a dance to the music of a violin and a big drum that an elderly man beats with a stick; singing accompanies them. The dance is not unlike square dancing, which I'm familiar with. The participants—who include a number of elderly men and women—are made up mainly of young people, and since I know most of them (the girls more than the boys, to be honest, because of the Sunday boat trips) I feel right at home. One of the family, if I might be so bold. I see us as equals, like relatives, and they don't make me feel like an outsider, far from it.

The men stay outside by their fires, drinking and talking loudly, which isn't like them; occasionally tempers flare. It's said that "Indians" can't hold their liquor—is there any truth to that? I can't, in any case. I'm not used to it, and I have to rush behind the dance hall to throw up on a little spruce tree. I have a great time, late into the night, so much so that I sleep in until midway through Sunday afternoon. Back in the village the party lasts until Sunday night.

André and I go to the Hudson's Bay store on the Monday morning to buy motor oil, since the plane that was supposed to bring us some is running a week late. We're greeted by a strange sight: every able-bodied man in the village is walking around slowly, bent double, sometimes reaching down to pick something up off the ground. They're gathering up bottles, Mr. Lloyd explains, along with bottle caps, and the odd glass shard, so they can dispose of them in the lake, far from shore. They're worried the RCMP might stop by for a visit, which is always possible. The scene leaves its mark on me; I think the men look like guilty children who don't want to be caught red-handed. It hurts me to see the scars of a profound injustice.*

And while we're getting ahead of ourselves… Round about 2015 I used Google Earth to revisit the area around Waswanipi and Gull Lake. That feeling I had of being encircled by civilization on the way back from Desmaraisville turned out to be something of a premonition: now there are big, irregular fields there, linked by roads, a shade of green lighter than the rest of the forest they nibble away at. Cutovers that often leave behind only thin strips of trees by waterways. The peat bogs are spared, of course. Zooming in on the satellite photo you can make out darker streaks at regular intervals: windrows of branches taken over by the raspberry bushes. I saw the same thing on the ground, east of Baston Reservoir. If the forest around Gull Lake was part of a traditional hunting ground, it's nothing short of catastrophic.

---

* I still didn't know about the realities of residential schools, of how children would be taken away and given up for adoption abroad!

The moccasins Mrs. Gull made for me never leave my feet. Made from fawn-coloured leather, they give off a lovely smell of wood-smoke, and have traditional patterns on the top: flowers embroidered with coloured glass beads. The thin sole transforms the sole of the foot into an organ with its own sense of touch, protecting the skin from sharp or pointed rocks while allowing the wearer to feel every obstacle, to walk in the forest as silently as an animal. When I gave her the four bricks of tea the following week, Mrs. Gull, visibly delighted, took me by the arm as she thanked me, then went out to give one of the bricks to her neighbour, who we heard shriek with pleasure. A relative or a friend? I can guess that being able to share the gift makes it all the more precious in her eyes.

Tommy, meanwhile, has given me one of the four pups from his dog's litter. I've named him Moush, short for *atimoush*. I've realized that the village dogs go down to the lake at dusk and line up perfectly still in the water. The walleye follow the minnows in to the shore in the darkness, and from time to time a dog will plunge its head into the lake and bring it out again, a fish wriggling in its mouth. It will then run to shore, followed by its closest neighbours. And so I give Moush walleye to eat, along with table scraps and little things that André cooks for him.

Summer is drawing to a close, and we stay back at the camp to prepare the equipment for winter. The two months have gone by like a flash, and we're starting to feel nostalgic. The week before I'm to leave, Tommy asks if I'd like to spend the winter with him and his wife on their hunting ground. Just as I was thinking it would take me many more months, if not years, to get to the heart of the Cree soul. And yet my head goes light as I realize I've come to a fork in the road, that my destiny is being decided. At first I'm tempted to take him up on the offer, but I end up backing away from the unknown. To justify the decision in my own eyes, as well as Tommy's, I point out that I've already paid for the first trimester at the university college in Rouyn, and that my future will depend on these studies. What I don't say is that I'm missing my girlfriend, who is not afraid to go to remote places.

The farewells are brief but heartfelt, each of us feeling as though we'll never see each other again. With Moush on my lap, I watch crestfallen as the village grows smaller beneath the Cessna's wing, the shoreline we explored around the lake. Then the forest reasserts itself. I've refused to dive into the unknown, but the road ahead has not been traced ahead of time; chance is king, the unexpected reigns.

Proof of this awaits me in Amos. Just as in Radiguet's novel *The Devil in the Flesh*, my sweetheart has gone and found herself another man. "You were gone for two months, and now you're leaving for college again until Christmas. I can't spend all my life waiting. I can't just wither on the vine. I want to get married and leave home." She was sixteen! Those words did away with any vague desire to win back her heart, and I felt like I'd had a narrow escape.

College was hardly any better. I was kicked out just before the holidays, after my arrest when the police raided the Moulin Rouge bar. Still not twenty, I wasn't old enough to be hanging around drinking establishments when I should have been fast asleep in my room. I can't have been the first to have tried my luck: the police had a list of students from the college. But there I was, woken up at three o'clock in the morning. The head of discipline didn't bother lecturing me (as far as he was concerned, I was no doubt beyond all possible redemption in any case, especially since I didn't play any team sports...). I was to pack my bags and leave the college after breakfast. Time enough for him to let my parents know...

I worked all winter as a clerk at a logging camp on the road to Matagami, occasionally thinking that, further to the east, the Gulls were laying traps on their hunting ground. Although I got emotional just thinking of them, I had no regrets. So what if I didn't complete my classical education? Maybe things were better that way: what use would that pre-packaged education have been when I wanted to pursue a career as a writer?

I would learn what I deemed necessary by myself, following the advice of Hemingway, who said that novelists were to learn on the job, to draw on a wide variety of experiences. At the logging camp I discovered the lives of men who make a living felling trees in the snow and the cold, a job that my grandfather and my father had done, along with several of my uncles.

Perhaps because my family often moved and each time this involved changing our friends and surroundings, from a young age I made my peace with the unknown, with the unexpected, with sheer chance.

"I shouldn't have done that... If only I'd taken such-and-such a path..." Going over the past like this is absurd: we have become who we are through the sum of our experiences, because of the choices made day after day, some of them insignificant, others sending us off in a different direction. If we had made different decisions at a given moment, we would be different today: it is important to realize that we have lived a life in keeping with who we are. Looking back and rebuilding our lives is nothing but a waste of time and energy. Instead, we must remain connected to the present moment, looking to the future, attentive to the blind chance that is our master. Looking back on the past should serve only to shed light on the choices that present themselves. It's what we call "experience."

5

1967, Schefferville. I was an "accountant" at the only bank in town, or rather the assistant to the manager in charge of lending and public relations; for my part I managed the thirteen employees and day-to-day operations. Lots of customers would stop by the counter next to my desk to have me work out their little problems. After two months the bank manager, Jack Warner (who didn't speak a word of French), pointed out that the "Indians" would often come to me for advice. And yet I didn't treat them any differently from other clients, although that might have explained it.

I didn't know all of them, but they knew me, and I was one of the rare White men who was able to go to the Montagnais* and Naskapi reserves without children throwing stones at my car. Dyed-in-the-wool atheist though I was, I enjoyed going to Sunday mass in Innu at the little chapel decorated with elements from the natural world. It reminded me of Waswanipi and the missionary I had met there: Jean Ibbotson, the blonde angel.

One day I'm serving an Innu customer at the counter when a man walks up and tosses his bank book down on the papers that are spread out in front of us.

"Get me one hundred dollars!" he snaps.

I flick the book back over to him:

"Please wait your turn, I'm serving a customer."

Livid with anger, he picks up the book and storms into the manager's office without knocking. I see Mr. Warner sidle up behind me, tail between his legs, go over to the tills, and dash back with a handful of bills. The customer leaves, not without staring daggers at me first. Warner tells me at closing time that

---

*   As the Innu have been known since the start of the French colony.

I snubbed the boss who runs the mine, which is to say he runs our town.

"Boss or not, he is a vulgar asshole," I shrug.

A retort that left my boss speechless. He never brought up the incident again, but the story must have made it back to the "Indians" because they all started to say hello every time they walked past my counter. And when I would go fishing on weekends with my little Bridgestone motorcycle, Innu families down by the lake fishing for lake trout, or simply enjoying a Sunday picnic by the fire, would invite me to share their meal. That's how I tasted porcupine roasted whole on the spit, so that the fire burned the quills; it smelled of singed hair, but once the black crust had been broken, the meat was juicy and tender.

6

Montreal, the late 2000s. On my way into the office, I catch the end of a radio interview with a very eloquent man belonging to the First Nations, a lawyer and member of a United Nations committee in Geneva. Being a publisher who's always on the lookout for a book in the making, I contact this Romeo Saganash to propose that he write a book about his life experiences, the claims being made by the Crees, or what he expects from other Quebecers. He's interested and offers to meet me the following week in the lobby of a hotel on what he calls "Boulevard Ti-Poil," meaning Boulevard René-Lévesque.

At this stage I still haven't made the connection between him and William Saganash, thinking that the name must be as common among the Crees as Vollant or Mackenzie among the Innu, or Tremblay or Nguyen in Montreal. At half past six in the evening I arrive at the place we agreed on. I haven't had time to look up his photo online, but I say to myself that I'll have no trouble recognizing a Cree in a Montreal hotel. Surprise! The lobby has been overtaken by the Assembly of First Nations Quebec-Labrador.

I'll give Romeo a call from the front desk, I thought. But first I cast my eyes over the crowd; it could be a group of mayors chatting to each other at a conference or professionals at a training day. And suddenly an image comes to me, a vision that comes down to settle over reality: the men of Waswanipi hunting for beer bottles and caps on a Monday morning. The contrast is striking, and I see how far the First Nations have come in forty years.

A man pulls away from the group and goes to sit in an armchair. I recognize him! Go over to him.

"Romeo Saganash? Jean-Yves Soucy."

He stands to shake my hand. We'd used each others' first names on the telephone and we keep going like that.

"Are you William's son? You look a lot like him."

He opens his eyes wide in astonishment. I explain the context in which I met his father in 1963, and we sit down and talk some more about that, forgetting all about the book.

"It's the first time I've ever met anyone who knew my father and the old village, apart from my older brothers and the elders," he says.

He has no memories at all of the village by the lake, very few of his father, who died when he was seven; back then he was at the residential school in La Tuque and neither he nor his brothers were able to go to the funeral, the school having no budget to cover the expense. Piecing the dates together, I realize he was the smiling two-year-old I enjoyed playing with. I also learn that the Hudson's Bay post closed in 1965 and that the village was moved twenty-five kilometres up the Waswanipi River, close to the road that leads to Chibougamau.

After I fill him in on my experiences as a young fire warden in 1963, Romeo tells me his life story as an adult. After becoming a lawyer, he was deputy grand chief of the Grand Council of the Crees, he played an active role in the negotiations leading to the Peace of the

Braves agreement (La Paix des Braves) signed between the Crees and the Quebec government, and he made an important contribution to developing the United Nations Declaration on the Rights of Indigenous Peoples. He lives in Quebec City, where he represents the Grand Council of the Crees with the Quebec government, a kind of unofficial ambassador. I think he's inherited his father's innate sense of diplomacy.

As I listen to him, I think that William would have been so proud of his youngest son, and happy to see that he was right: education would help the Crees stand up for their rights and assert their claims. While William would make the trip from Waswanipi to James Bay, his son now spoke four languages and was travelling the world. It will have taken no more than a few generations for the Crees to take themselves in hand, to begin coming up with a new way to live on their lands, to marry tradition with progress. Not everything is perfect, far from it. There are still many problems facing their communities, but at least they have taken control of their own destiny.

A member of the New Democratic Party, Romeo will even be elected (and re-elected)

to represent Abitibi–Baie-James–Nunavik–
Eeyou in Ottawa. Born at a time when he
was still a second-class citizen, when his own
people distrusted federal civil servants, now he
is one of the men and women who pass laws
and run the country. What an example he has
set, but at what cost!

Romeo Saganash and I hit it off in the hotel
lobby. Over the course of the conversation he
makes it clear that I got to know Waswanipi
just before things changed drastically for the
Crees.

"You have to write that, Jean-Yves," he tells
me. "About your relationship with my father
and the others, how you saw the village. You
got to see the end of an era."

"Your father could sense it was coming…
But I'm no ethnologist. What gives me the
right to talk about the Crees?"

"You were seeing things with fresh eyes,
and you were genuinely interested and respectful, that's why my father and Tommy became
friends with you. Just talk about your experiences. You're a writer, after all."

He has to go back to his meeting. We'll be in touch a few times again after this, but nothing will come of his book because neither I nor he will manage to get a grant that would allow him to write it as his leisure. And then he became an MP.

My book will be written, simply called *Waswanipi*.

Epilogue

2013. Baie-Trinité. Now retired I spend my summers with my wife on Quebec's North Shore. Before I read *Le Journal de Québec* (from the day before!) in the village restaurant, I stop by the fishway, a daily pilgrimage that will surely earn me a plenary indulgence or two in fishing heaven. No visitors, just the student at the logging station. We have our usual chat, then I go up to the top of the dam to peer down at the water below.

A van pulls into the parking lot and a gaggle of kids streams out, four of them making a break for the steps. A man and a woman follow them out of the van and start to stretch. The children have me surrounded: two boys around ten or twelve, a nine-year-old girl, and the youngest boy, around six years old. Innu.

The oldest asks me what I'm looking at; I pass him my polarized sunglasses that eliminate the water's glare.

"Salmon. Look carefully and you can see them swim."

Thirty seconds later he cries out with joy:

"There!" he tells his brother.

He takes off the glasses, hesitates and gives me a glance, and, as I nod my agreement, passes them to the younger brother. The father comes to join us, and I'm struck by the love in his eyes as he looks at his children. Then he turns to me and smiles as he holds out a hand.

"André."

"Jean-Yves."

I wonder if that's his first or last name, but it doesn't matter. The little girl who's just had her turn with the glasses passes them to her father who spots the salmon and describes the show in Innu for his children. Then he hands them back the glasses. I'm again struck by how close the Innu and Cree languages are, just as I was when I arrived in Schefferville, less than four years after my stay in Waswanipi.

"Do you speak Innu at home?"

"Always. Just not when they're doing their homework."

"It's important to keep one's language."

"My wife and I see to it."

The oldest boy, who hasn't strayed far from us, has overheard and asks me:

"Why is a language important?"

At last a chance to play at being teacher!

"A language brings with it traces of the past and a way of looking at the world. We think with our language, and to be an Innu you need to think in Innu. Language binds us to all those who came before us. Take a word in Innu: one day maybe ten or twenty generations ago one of your ancestors came up with it because he needed it to say something. That word is like an echo from that ancestor. The elders gave you these words, a language to understand the world and to put it into words. It's a valuable legacy that must be preserved. Your language is part of who you are."

I stop, give him a smile, and ask:

"Does that answer your question or do you want some more where that came from?"

"No, no, I understand. Thank you."

Then he goes back to his siblings and asks for the glasses.

"That was nice what you just said. I'm going to use that," says André.

"Go for it. I didn't come up with it all myself. I must have read some of it somewhere or other. But it's true for everyone, whatever their language."

He nods, then looks over at the parking lot; his wife is talking away to the student. We chat, too, resting our elbows against the guardrail. André lives in Mingan (Ekuanitshit, no doubt, but he doesn't say) and is working on the Romaine dam; they're just back from a few days at the Valcartier Vacation Village. The family seems quite well-off, apparently spared the problems of violence and abuse that are unfortunately common in a number of First Nations communities. André is encouraging his children to study.

"That way they'll have more options in life."

He tells his children it's time to hit the road again and turns to me:

"We still have more than three hundred kilometres to go."

The oldest boy gives me back my sunglasses and thanks me. André and I shake hands again.

"Good luck to you."

"Good luck with your fishing."

I watch them go back to their gleaming van, thinking to myself that they've been uprooted, not from their lands, but from their way of life. And yet, before my very eyes, I can see they're managing to reinvent themselves, to lay down new markers in a world that has completely changed on them. And they're doing that without turning their backs on what they are: a unique facet of human diversity.

Afterword

I saw William, my father, for the final time, unrecognizable, in his hospital bed in Lebel-sur-Quévillon. I was seven years old.

I remember, because while I realized he would soon be leaving us, I was also about to leave myself, for residential school. I know that he knew just by the way he looked at me that day, a look of such absolute sadness that upset me so much. What was he thinking? What was he thinking? It's a question that haunts me to this day: What was he thinking?

Perhaps he wanted to tell me something one last time, but what was it? What was it?

Today I am the same age as he was when he left us, an accomplished man. When I was young—I didn't know why at the time—I was obsessed with his craftsman's hands, sculpted by time and effort, laced with veins. Spring, summer, fall, or winter, I admired him like a child awaiting his turn to be like his father. Like him building canoes, like him patiently crafting perfect snowshoes that I still consider to be works of art, like him carving his paddles and all the other tools he needed to live the traditional Cree life. He loved and had a deep knowledge of his boreal forest, especially his Broadback Valley.

I was born quite literally on his hunting ground, in a tent, in the early 1960s, by what was one of his favourite lakes (because it was teeming with so many different species of fish): Théodat Lake, which the Crees have known for thousands of years as *Mishagomish* (meaning "big little lake"). Despite the short period of time I spent with my father, I still believe I inherited some of his character, his generosity, his openness to the Other, and, if only a little, his wisdom.

One day as we left our spring hunting ground for the place where we would spend the summer, I remember experiencing a bitter disappointment. Sitting in the middle of the canoe, my mother up front, my father behind, I managed to take out a monarch butterfly in mid-air with my slingshot! An exploit, I figured, that was deserving of admiration from the man I wanted to be when I grew up. Not a word! I knew that he had seen me, but he flat out ignored me, no matter how I pestered him: "*Dji Wabmiin a? Dji Wabmiin a?* Did you see that?" No reaction! Needless to say, I felt crushed for the remainder of that trip as we paddled on to where we would spend the night. I was around five years old, and I didn't understand. I couldn't understand, I suppose.

Sadly, I never got the chance to talk about it with him.

It wasn't until some thirty years later that my mother, who spoke only Cree, reminded me of that moment as we chatted over a plate of moose shoulder roast.

"Do you remember?"

"I do, Nabesh (as she would sometimes call me), and if you're still wondering why today, then it's high time you realized he gave you something precious. We spoke that night, and his hope (*boukshaiitoumoun*) was that you would one day understand. Like all good hunters, he didn't want you to grow up to be boastful. He wanted you to stay humble, whatever the situation. His sorrow at being obliged to say nothing, to do nothing, his silence was his response. You being stupid enough to kill a butterfly for no reason is another matter entirely. If I'd been him, I'd have made you eat it!"

It was a lesson in humility, which is my greatest strength today.

Back when I was a child, every young Cree dreamed of living the traditional life, of pursuing the age-old traditions, of absorbing all the knowledge handed down from generation to generation about the environment, about time, about why we have six seasons, about the animal world, about the plants and fruits that healed so many of my passing ailments; in short, about the reason we call her Mother Earth.

When I left the residential school in La Tuque after a decade, I promised myself two things. First, I would go back into the bush to live a life of hunting, fishing, trapping, and gathering once again. And so, for two years I walked in the footsteps of my father William and my ancestors who are buried on these lands. Then I swore to myself instinctively, without knowing how, that I would make my peace with the men and women who had shut me away in that linguistic, cultural, and political prison. Linguistic, because in those places that were tasked with assimilating us, speaking one's indigenous language wasn't allowed. Cultural, because that federal policy was also intended to tear indigenous children away from their culture, their land, their language, their parents, and their communities. And political, lastly, for the sole reason that we were "Indians." Under the Indian Act, our parents faced imprisonment if they didn't comply. Such was the "law" at the time. Once he'd left with all the children from the village, the agent working for the Department of Indian Affairs doubtless knew nothing of the terrible silence left behind in those villages devoid of the laughter and joy of children. It pains me to relate what my mother Mary Jane had to say on the matter. Suffice it to say that I can't imagine how I could go on living if I were told that my three children had become, without my consent, wards of the state.

From that carpet of fir branches in a tent on the shores of the Mishagomish, I eventually grew up to become a Member of Canada's Parliament. There, my attempt to make my peace failed. But that's another, as yet unfinished, story.

Among my large family of sisters and brothers, Wally was most like my father, in every respect. On the day of my eighteenth birthday, we found ourselves in a bar in Desmaraisville, chatting about the future. Back then the tiny village of barely ten souls had not one, not two, but three bars. The reason for their existence was, of course, the surrounding mines. But that's beside the point. What I wanted to know is whether Wally could teach me all that my father had taught him. His answer crushed me.

"I can teach you everything he taught me, but it will always be me who will have given you that, not our father."

Ouch! Wally was right.

While his remark hurt, it also strengthened my resolve. With the main provider for the family, the community, and the nation no longer with us, how were we to provide for ourselves today, as he had done? How might I continue his legacy? How might *I* act as he had done, differently but to the same end: to be a provider?

And so I negotiated agreements on behalf of my community, for my nation, to provide for people in my own fashion. I often wonder if my own fate changed with my father's. Was my own journey of more than forty years ultimately determined solely by his death? I often ask myself these questions, and others, too. I would have liked to have had the chance to thank Jean-Yves Soucy while he was still alive for this account, not only for having honoured William's memory but for reminding us how things were back then, in the early days of our relationships with such different peoples. Soucy makes us realize the extent to which the region's development has taken off since his first trip there. I, too, pay tribute to his memory.

I began by recounting the last time I saw my father, on his deathbed. Several of my sisters and brothers were there. William was barely recognizable—his cancer had spread—and he could no longer speak or move; the right side of his body was paralyzed. One moment from our visit will stay with me for the rest of my life. A look of sheer panic—I remember it well—suddenly came over my father. He tried to tell us something, but the words never left his mouth. Seconds later the sheets that covered his now-frail body turned yellow with urine. I ran out of his room, fell to my knees in the hallway, in tears, devastated to see the man who had always stood so tall in my child's eyes, the greatest hunter of all time, so helpless.

That was the last time I saw William.

Romeo Saganash
March 2020

Note from the Publisher

Kevin Brousseau, who is from Waswanipi and holds a Masters Degree in Linguistics from the Université du Québec à Montréal, kindly agreed to reread the manuscript and review the language and the words in Cree. He provided this glossary with explanations regarding the meaning, the alphabet, and the particular dialect used in Waswanipi.

There is no recognized standard for spelling this Cree dialect using the Latin alphabet. However, a standard spelling system based on the internal workings of the language's phonology and morphology has been developed in the western provinces and so this is what is used below in the second column. The third column provides the Cree spelling that is actually in use in Waswanipi.

Word or words with page numbers	Cree Spelling #1	Cree Spelling #2	Meaning
Waswanipi	Wâswânipiy	ᐙᓵᓂᐱᕀ	Waswanipi does not mean "lights on the water" but rather Torch-fishing Lake/Lac pêche au flambeau.
muskeg p. 13			A Cree word used on the west side of James Bay, by peoples such as the Moose Cree or the Swampy Cree (maškekw) or the Plaines Cree (maskêk). The Algonquin term is related but different.
Gull Lake/lac au Goéland	Ciyâško-wacištoni-sâkahikan	ᒋᔮᔥᑯ ᐗᒋᔥᑐᓂ ᓵᑲᐦᐃᑲᓐ	Gull's nest lake
ochimaow p. 19	ocimâw	ᐅᒋᒫᐤ	A person in a position of authority.
misiou p. 20	mîsîw	ᒦᓰᐤ	He/she defecates.
tanta ochimaow p. 20	tânita ocimâw	ᑖᓂᑕ ᐅᒋᒫᐤ	Where is the person in charge?
wapistan p. 38	wâpištân	ᐚᐱᔥᑖᓐ	marten
massimakouish p. 39	mâsamekos	ᒫᓴᒣᑯᔅ	brook trout
nthkoyiniskwaw p. 39	natohkoyiniskwew	ᓇᑐᐦᑯᔨᓂᔅᑵᐤ	nurse
skwaw p. 39	iskwew	ᐃᔅᑵᐤ	woman
kawichihat nthkoyiniskwaw p. 39	kâ wîcihat natohkoyiniskwew	ᑳ ᐑᒋᐦᐊᐟ ᓇᑐᐦᑯᔨᓂᔅᑵᐤ	The nurse you are helping.
Wapanisou p. 40	Wâpanisiw	ᐚᐸᓂᓯᐤ	The personification of the east wind, the god of the east wind.
Shawanisou p. 40	Šâwanisiw	ᔖᐗᓂᓯᐤ	The personification of the south wind, the god of the south wind.
Chiwatinmisou p. 40	Cîwetinisiw	ᒌᐍᑎᓂᓯᐤ	The personification of the north wind, the god of the north wind.
mistapéou p. 40	mištâpew	ᒥᔥᑖᐯᐤ	Literally, "big man," a supernatural being thought to communicate with a person who divines by use of the shaking tent.
Waskaganish p. 41	Wâskâhikaniš	ᐚᔅᑳᐦᐃᑲᓂᔥ	Literally, "small fort."

kwé or kwei p. 50	kwey	·ᑫᔨ	Greetings.
mous... napamous p. 50	môs^w... nâpe-môs^w	ᒍᐧ..., ᐧᐁ ᐯ ᒍᐧ	moose, buck
mischisin p. 51	mascisin	ᒪᔆᒉᓯᐊ	moccasin
mouswiyanmichisin p. 51	môsowayâni- mascisin	ᒍᔆᐧᐊᔾᓂ ᒪᔆᒉᔆᐊ	moose hide moccasin
oush, sh or *ish* p. 51	oš, š, ou iš		Suffix indicating something small.
atim p. 51	atim^w	ᐊᑎᒍ	dog
atimoush p. 51	atimoš	ᐊᑎᒍᔕ	puppy
inhin p. 51	ehe	ᐯᐦᐯ	yes
nipiou p. 51	nâpew	ᐧᐁ ᐁ	man
napamous p. 52	nâpe-môs^w	ᐧᐁ ᐯ ᒍᐧ	moose, buck
nousamous p. 52	nôše-môs^w	ᐧᐳᔕ ᒍᐧ	moose, cow
nipi p. 52	nipiy	ᓂ ᐱ ᔨ	water
nipi p. 52	nîpiy	ᓈ ᐱ ᔨ	leaf
sipi p. 52	sîpiy, sîpiy-h	ᓯ ᐱ ᔨ, ᓯ ᐱ ᔨᐦ	river, rivers
Eeyouch, Eeyou	Iyiyiwac, Iyiyiw	ᐃ ᔩ ᔨ ᐧᐊᐦ, ᐃ ᔩ ᔨ ᐤ	Cree people. Note: This word is not used in Waswanipi where
Iyiyouch, Iyiyou p. 52			we say: Iyiniwac/ᐃ ᔨ ᓂ ᐧᐊᐦ (pronounced ee-nooch)
yotinipiyou P. 57	yôtinipayiw	ᔫᑎᓂ ᐸ ᔨ ᐤ	a sudden wind
outchek p. 59	ocek	ᐅᒉᐦ	fisher
Pasho otchimasquaw, Johnny p. 60	pešiw ocimâskwew	ᐯ ᔫᐤ ᐅᒉᒫᔆᑫᐤ	Bring the boss's wife, Johnny.
mishagomish p. 100	Mešikamîš	ᒉ ᔆᑲᒦᔕ	Little big lake.
Dji Wabmiin a? Dji Wabmiin a? p. 101	Ci wâpamin-â? Ci wâpamin-â?	ᒋ ·ᐧᐊᐸᒥᓂ ᐧᐊᐦ? ᒋ ·ᐧᐊᐸᒥᓂ ᐧᐊᐦ?	Did you see that?
Nabesh p. 101	nâpešiš	ᐧᐁ ᐯ ᔫᔕ	Nickname given to Romeo Saganash by his mother
boukshaiitoumoun p. 101	pakoseyihtamowin	ᐸᑯ ᔫᐦᑕᒧᐧᐃᐊ	hope

Also from Baraka Books

Exile Blues
Douglas Gary Freeman

Things Worth Burying
Matt Mayr

Fog
Rana Bose

The Daughters' Story
Murielle Cyr

Yasmeen Haddad Loves Joanasi Maqaittik
Carolyn Marie Souaid

The Nickel Range Trilogy by Mick Lowe
The Raids
The Insatiable Maw
Wintersong

NONFICTION

Stolen Motherhood, Surrogacy and Made-to-Order Children
Maria De Koninck

Still Crying for Help, The Failure of Our Mental Healthcare Services
Sadia Messaili

A Distinct Alien Race, The Untold Story of Franco-Americans
David Vermette

*The Einstein File, The FBI's Secret War
on the World's Most Famous Scientist*
Fred Jerome

Journey to the Heart of the First Peoples Collections
Marie-Paule Robitaille

Let's Move On
Paul Okalik with Louis McComber

Patriots, Traitors and Empires, The Story of Korea's Struggle for Freedom
Stephen Gowans

Printed by Imprimerie Gauvin
Gatineau, Québec